GREAT MARQUES POSTER BOOK

M.G.

CHRIS HARVEY

OCTOPUS BOOKS

Contents

Introduction	**4**	
1925 Old Number One	5	1946 TC Midget	27
1930 M-type Midget	7	1952 TD Midget	29
1932 C-type Midget	9	1955 TF Midget 1500	31
1932 F-type Magna	11	1956 ZA Magnette	33
1933 J2 Midget	13	1959 MGA 1600 roadster	35
1933 K3 Magnette	15	1963 Midget 1098	37
1934 NA Magnette	17	1967 MGB roadster	39
1934 NA Magnette supercharged	19	1968 MGC roadster	41
1934 PA Midget Cream Cracker	21	1973 MGB GT V8	43
1937 TA Midget	23	1980 MGB roadster	45
1938 SA saloon	25	1982 MG Metro	47

First published in 1985 by Octopus Books Limited, 59 Grosvenor Street, London W1

© 1985 Octopus Books Limited

ISBN 0 7064 2340 2

Produced by Mandarin Publishers Limited, 22a Westlands Road, Quarry Bay, Hong Kong

Printed in Hong Kong

Acknowledgements
Cars provided by BL Heritage Ltd (page 5), Keith J. Portsmore (7), Allan Bentley (9), Elwin S. Sapcote (11), Paradise Garage (13), Briggs Cunningham Museum (15), B. Hague Sutton (17), Mike Allison (19), Bob Williams (21), Alastair Naylor/Keith Storey (23), Michael Turvill (25), Alastair Naylor/Derek Farley (3, 27), Alastair Naylor/Jack Tordoff (29), Alastair Naylor/Vicki Fell (31), Warren Marsh (33), Simon Robinson/Harold Corkhill (35), J.A. Tassell (37), E.F. Williams (39), Richard Tasker (41), Barry Sidery-Smith (43), Performance Cars Ltd (45), BL Cars Limited (47).

Page 1 The famous M.G. octagon.
Page 3 1946 M.G.TC.

Special photography: Ian Dawson and Chris Linton

Introduction

People have been falling in love with M.G.s for more than 60 years. This is because they have always been cheap but cheerful sporting cars, placing the excitement of high-speed motoring within the grasp of the ordinary man and woman. They have always been eminently practical cars, too, with a great reputation for reliability because they were based on well-tried components designed for rugged saloons.

The first M.G. designer was Cecil Kimber, manager of Morris Garages in Oxford, who felt he could produce something more glamorous than the Bullnose Morris he had to sell. Such cars could be sold at a higher profit than the standard models on which they were based. The first one, in 1922, had lowered suspension like a competition car and an open body with a special paint scheme. These models sold very well because the basic cars were very cheap to start with and by 1923 they were known as M.G.s – for Morris Garages – to distinguish them from the ordinary Morris.

Throughout the 1920s, M.G. production expanded as the parent firm, Morris Motors, swallowed its suppliers to become one of the biggest car makers in Britain. By 1930, M.G.s were selling in substantial quantities and production was moved from Oxford to a new factory at Abingdon, 10 km (six miles) away. Much of M.G.'s success was founded on the Midget, a sporting version of the pre-war Morris Minor, with an advanced overhead camshaft four-cylinder engine. It was during the five years that followed the move that technological advances ran riot at Abingdon with a stream of exquisite little cars, each of which bore less and less resemblance to the stolid, basic machines. Their successes in competition on road and track were countless and today every one is seen as something of a classic. But there were so many variants, and so much money was spent on development, that they proved not to be very profitable. The axe had to fall, and it was swung by Leonard Lord, a hard-headed production engineer working for the Nuffield Organization, which had been formed as an amalgamation of William Morris's numerous enterprises.

From 1935, M.G. had to stick far closer to their original cars, but their reputation had been firmly established during the glorious racing years of the early 30s. Until the outbreak of war in 1939, M.G.s fell into two categories: durable little sports cars that looked like the old road racers, and bigger sporting saloons.

Abingdon put in a marvellous war effort, building aircraft and tank parts, and thanks to a supremely loyal workforce was able to swing straight back into production with the pre-war M.G. Midget in 1945. Kimber had died that year, but his place was to be taken by a manager every bit as gifted, John Thornley, who had worked for M.G. before the war alongside a brilliant designer, Syd Enever.

The M.G. Midget had so much character that it was in great demand in the late 1940s, selling extremely well in America. Dealers there were so anxious to buy M.G.s that the importers made them take two Volkswagens for every Midget.

Every good thing has to come to an end, though, and the Midget was looking very dated by the time two rivals, Healey and Triumph, introduced new cars in 1952. By then, the Nuffield Organization had amalgamated with Austin to form the British Motor Corporation, with Leonard Lord (now of Austin) in charge – and still smarting at having been sacked by Morris. He took over the Healey project and forced Abingdon to shelve its new car.

It was only when M.G. sales began to suffer seriously in 1955 that the company was allowed to introduce the MGA, which promptly sold 100,000 models! During this period, from 1955 to 1962, Abingdon became the biggest sports car factory in the world, producing Austin-Healeys alongside their M.G.s

A new small Austin-Healey, called the Sprite, was re-badged as the M.G. Midget in 1961, and a new version of the MGA, the MGB, was introduced in 1962: they were meant to sell 850,000 between them during an 18-year production run.

This was too long, however, and throughout this period M.G. was denied essential investment as first BMC and then British Leyland struggled to produce saloon cars at a profit. Tragically, Abingdon – which had never known a strike and had produced cars cheaper than anywhere else in the empire – was closed in 1980, as British Leyland pruned savagely to produce a life-saving car, the Metro. Happily BL kept the name, and now the MG version of the Metro, produced at Longbridge, has come full circle as the top of a saloon car line.

1925 M.G. Old Number One

M.G. Old Number One

Ironically Old Number One is not the first M.G., but represents Cecil Kimber's first attempt to build a car from Morris parts specially for competition. It was given the title Old Number One by company publicity men in the 1930s when it was returned to Abingdon as the oldest M.G. they had seen. But such quibbles matter little: Old Number One, still proudly preserved by British Leyland Heritage, represents the spirit of the first M.G.s. Work started on it in the spring of 1924 when the first octagon-emblazoned M.G. advertisements appeared, showing that the new cars had become a marque distinct from Morris specials.

However, Old Number One was always very special because it was constructed for Kimber's use in the prestigious Land's End Trial, rather than for an ordinary customer. The rear end of its Morris Cowley chassis was sawn off and replaced by two special side rails to provide mountings for outrigged semi-elliptic springs. This modification was intended to give it better traction than a normal Bullnose Morris on the tortuous hills of the Land's End Trial.

The Morris motor company had also taken over one of its suppliers, Hotchkiss, who made engines, providing them with a particularly attractive overhead valve four-cylinder unit of 11.9 hp. It was an impressive engine that had been used in the Gilchrist car between 1920 and 1923, and soon found its way into the Morris special chassis as a way of providing more power and greater flexibility to combat those fearful hills. The power output of 35 bhp might not seem much by the standards of today, but it was three times that of the very successful Austin Seven introduced two years earlier, and the M.G. was only twice its capacity at 1548 cc. In many ways it is comparable with one of the 'homologation special' supercars of today, with extra large Morris Oxford brakes and ultra-lightweight coachwork by Carbodies of Coventry. This body was the absolute minimum that Kimber could get away with on the road. At least half of it was bonnet, with a skimpy two-seater cockpit and extremely small wings giving it a very purposeful appearance. This car achieved its target of a gold medal in the 1925 trial with Kimber at the wheel – who then sold it to a friend in Lancashire. Subsequently it was discovered in a scrapyard in Stockport, near Manchester, by an M.G. employee and returned to the works in 1932 – to be hailed as 'Old Number One'.

ENGINE		CHASSIS	
Type	11.9 hp Hotchkiss, in-line, water-cooled	Frame	Modified Morris Cowley, two side members, cross members
No. of cylinders	4		
Bore/stroke mm	69.5 × 102		
Displacement cc	1548	Wheelbase mm	2591
Valve operation	Overhead, pushrod	Track – front mm	1219
Sparkplugs per cyl.	1	Track – rear mm	1219
Compression ratio	5:1	Suspension – front	Half-elliptic springs, beam axle
Carburation	1 SU carburettor, air pressure fuel feed, hand pump	Suspension – rear	Half-elliptic springs, live axle
BHP	Approx. 35	Brakes	Morris Oxford drums front and rear
Transmission	Three-speed manual gearbox		

PERFORMANCE	
Maximum speed	129 km/h (80 mph)
Fuel consumption	14.13 litres/100 km (20 mpg)

1930 M.G. M-type Midget

M.G. M-type Midget

The emergent M.G. Car Company benefited greatly when William Morris took over the bankrupt firm of Wolseley in 1927. They had developed a brilliant little 8 hp four-cylinder overhead camshaft engine for a small car that Morris wanted to produce as a competitor to the all-conquering Austin Seven. However, this new Wolseley engine made a prototype Morris Minor perform so well that it was considered too fast for ordinary use! Morris had it detuned for the Minor, but Kimber managed to get hold of one of the higher-powered prototypes. He soon had it modified and rebodied along similar lines to Old Number One, to produce a nippy sports machine called the M.G. M-type. One of its most notable outward features was a radiator scaled down from one used on later versions of the bigger M.G. This distinctive design was so well received that it was to stay with the marque substantially unaltered for 25 years – and was then still to form the basis for later grilles.

The first M-type appeared at the 1928 London Motor Show, but it was hurriedly constructed and it would be six months before it could be put into production. Once it was readily available, though, it sold extremely well: a total of 3,235 in the following three years.

By then, Austin was producing very attractive sporting versions of the Seven, but in general terms the Midget (as the M-type was called) was technically superior. The overhead cam engine produced more power than the Austin side-valve unit and the extensive use of well-tried Morris Minor parts kept down the cost. The Minor chassis had a lowered steering column and springs, as well as a special gearchange. The body was as simple as possible to reduce costs. It was made from panels of plywood covered with fabric, which were mounted on a wooden frame – a method of construction that was very much in vogue at the time. The car had a traditional racing-style pointed boat tail, and a small 'V' windscreen which made the Midget look far more attractive than the average Austin Seven sports. Had Austin decided to make large numbers of these sporting two-seaters, rather than leaving the effort to specialists whose overheads were higher, the new Midget might have faced tougher competition.

But the fact was that it performed as well as it looked. With an all-up weight of only 499 kg (1,100 lb) it was as fast as the bigger M.G., while being very nimble with it. No wonder it was acclaimed as a 'real sports car'.

ENGINE		CHASSIS	
Type	M.G. in-line, water-cooled	Frame	Twin side members, cross members
No. of cylinders	4	Wheelbase mm	1980
Bore/stroke mm	57 × 83	Track – front mm	1070
Displacement cc	847	Track – rear mm	1070
Valve operation	Overhead camshaft	Suspension – front	Half-elliptic springs, beam axle
Sparkplugs per cyl.	1		
Compression ratio	6.2:1	Suspension – rear	Half-elliptic springs, live axle
Carburation	One SU carburettor		
BHP	Early 20, later 27	Brakes	Drums front and rear
Transmission	Three-speed manual gearbox		
		PERFORMANCE	
		Maximum speed	105 km/h (65 mph)
		Fuel consumption	7.06 litres/100 km (40 mpg)

1932 M.G. C-type Midget

M.G. C-type Midget

It was inevitable that enthusiasts would race the M.G. Midget in a manner pioneered by the Austin Sevens since the early 1920s. They did this quite successfully with a minimum of tuning, although works-prepared examples ran with anything up to one-third more power (achieved by work on the cylinder head). But the Midget and the Seven were not always directly comparable in international racing because the smallest class – dominated by the Seven – had a 750 cc limit. Thus a Midget might beat a Seven, but the Seven scooped the glory because it could win its class.

Early experiments with a short-stroke version of the overhead camshaft engine showed that a great deal more power could be extracted by using higher revs, even in smaller-capacity form. Indeed several world records were captured from Austin by a highly-tuned example driven by Capt. George Eyston. This Midget had a streamlined body and supercharger, however, so again the publicity value was reduced. Kimber therefore decided that a more durable version of this car's 747 cc engine should be fitted to a Midget that looked like a road car. This would be called the Montlhéry Midget (after the French track where the records were broken), or the C-type, for competition. Like the rival Austin Seven

Ulster model, it could be bought with or without a supercharger.

No less than 14 of these new Midgets were built for the Brooklands Double Twelve race in 1931. And almost the entire staff of the factory was on hand to see their cars take the first five places in this race and the coveted team prize. It was heralded as one of the greatest triumphs by a single make in the history of motor racing – made even more extraordinary by the fact that it was the model's debut. More was to come, however, as Montlhéry Midget driver Norman Black won both the Irish Grand Prix and the Tourist Trophy in Ulster – which, with the Double Twelve, made up the three most important races in the United Kingdom that season. In all 44 of these cars were built by mid-1932, and they achieved a long string of competition successes, including victory in the Junior Car Club's 500-mile race at Brooklands, and that year breaking the world standing-start mile and kilometre records. Although they looked very much like normal Midgets, C types were readily-distinguishable by their cutaway doors (so that the occupants could lean out during hectic cornering), and asbestos-wrapped exhaust pipes (to save them from burning themselves!).

ENGINE			CHASSIS	
Type	M.G. in-line, water-cooled		Frame	Twin side members, cross members
No. of cylinders	4		Wheelbase mm	2060
Bore/stroke mm	57 × 73		Track – front mm	1070
Displacement cc	746		Track – rear mm	1070
Valve operation	Overhead camshaft		Suspension – front	Half-elliptic springs, beam axle
Sparkplugs per cyl.	1			
Compression ratio	5:1 – 6.5:1		Suspension – rear	Half-elliptic springs, live axle
Carburation	Various SU carburettors, also Powerplus supercharger		Brakes	Drums front and rear
			PERFORMANCE	
BHP	50–70		Maximum speed	121–137 km/h (75–85 mph)
Transmission	Four-speed manual gearbox		Fuel consumption	14.13–9.42 litres/100 km (20–30 mpg)

1932 M.G. F-type Magna

M.G. F-type Magna

The large six-cylinder cars made by M.G. from 1928 sold quite well, and it became apparent that there might be a market for a smaller 'six', combining the virtues of a very smooth-running engine with the attractive price of a miniature car. As a result, the F-type Magna was introduced late in 1931, to cause immediate confusion in M.G. nomenclature! To the dedicated M.G. follower it was all quite simple: the Midget was naturally an M-type, with the competition version being a C-type, and an updated version the D-Type. Experimental models bore EX-designations, making them, in turn, E-types. Therefore the next in line became the F-type – in this case with a chassis derived from the C-type's sliding trunnion rear suspension type. Meanwhile the D-type introduced at the same time had basically the same chassis as a C-type, but retained the M-type's cheaper, lower-powered, engine.

In effect, the F-type's engine was simply a six-cylinder version of the four-cylinder M-type unit. Its origins were disguised by a steel surround for the crankcase to make it look more glamorous. The name Magna followed on quite naturally as a bigger version of the Midget. Apart from having the six-cylinder overhead camshaft engine, shared with the Wolseley Hornet, the F-type Magna also had a four-speed C-type gearbox in marked contrast to the D-type's cheaper three-speed unit. It also had a longer wheelbase to accommodate the larger engine and to make room for two small rear seats. The performance was not outstanding when compared to the C-type because the engine's extra power over the M-type was largely negated by the extra weight, and so the F-type sold well as a touring, rather than a competition, machine. Nevertheless, one of Britain's greatest pre-war racing drivers, Dick Seaman, drove one in his first international competition, the 1932 Alpine Trial. The 1,250 Magnas made between 1931 and 1932 carried two distinct body styles, one the open four-seater and the other a close-coupled fixed-head coupé. The engine was exceptionally smooth in operation and the ride better than a normal Midget because of the longer wheelbase; the handling was as good as ever. Its relatively mundane performance matters little to enthusiasts today as they admire the exquisite workmanship that went into all these cars produced at Abingdon and Oxford in the period leading up to the Second World War.

ENGINE		CHASSIS	
Type	M.G. in-line, water-cooled	Frame	Twin side members, cross members
No. of cylinders	6	Wheelbase mm	2390
Bore/stroke mm	57 × 83	Track – front mm	1070
Displacement cc	1271	Track – rear mm	1070
Valve operation	Overhead camshaft	Suspension – front	Half-elliptic springs, beam axle
Sparkplugs per cyl.	1		
Compression ratio	6.2:1	Suspension – rear	Half-elliptic springs, live axle
Carburation	Two SU carburettors		
BHP	37	Brakes	Drums front and rear
Transmission	Four-speed manual gearbox		
		PERFORMANCE	
		Maximum speed	113 km/h (70 mph)
		Fuel consumption	8.56 litres/100 km (33 mpg)

1933 M.G. J2 Midget

M.G. J2 Midget

To add to the confusion over type designations, M.G. jumped several letters of the alphabet for some inexplicable reason when they introduced the next Midget, the J-type, in 1932. The best explanation so far offered is that J stood for Junior. Whatever the solution, the two-seater version, the J2, was instantly recognized as an absolute classic, and without a doubt one of the most attractive M.G.s ever made. Its revised body lines were derived directly from racing practice with deep cutaway doors like those used on the C-type. A double hump scuttle also came, with modifications, from the C-type along with a fold-flat windscreen and – initially – cycle-type wings. The cut-off tail followed late C-type practice with a large external, Le Mans-style, fuel tank carrying a spare wheel strapped on in a manner made popular in the reliability trials which preceded modern rallying. Later J-type Midgets had long sweeping front wings and more graceful rear wings, although both styles of bodywork are generally considered to be among the prettiest ever made. It is significant that this was the car which set the classic M.G. style that survived until 1955.

So far as the running gear was concerned, the J-type's chassis came from the D-type with a production version of the C-type's engine providing nearly as much power as the larger F-type could call on. It also had a new four-speed gearbox like the one installed in the Magna. Other versions of the J-type followed the same lines, with the J1 as a four-seater and the J3 as a supercharged version of the J2. The J4, although again very similar, was an outright racing car with improved steering and brakes. A total of 2,083 J2s was made from midway through 1932 until early 1934.

One of the main technical features of the J2 was a crossflow eight-port cylinder head which produced nearly as much power as the C-type, and achieved it at the very high revs (for 1932) of 5500. The lifespan of its two-bearing crankshaft could be decidedly slender, but the thrill of a car that responded and sounded like a racing machine seemed to make up for that! The J2, with its nimble handling and howling engine, rapidly became a favourite mount in all forms of competition motoring for years to come. The pure competition versions, notably the J4, were exceptionally fast, lapping Brooklands at more than 160 km/h (100 mph): their engines were, if anything, too fast for their chassis.

ENGINE		CHASSIS	
Type	M.G. in-line, water-cooled	Frame	Twin side-members, cross members
No. of cylinders	4	Wheelbase mm	2184
Bore/stroke mm	57 × 83	Track – front mm	1067
Displacement cc	847	Track – rear mm	1067
Valve operation	Overhead camshaft	Suspension – front	Half-elliptic springs, beam axle
Sparkplugs per cyl.	1		
Compression ratio	6.2:1	Suspension – rear	Half-elliptic springs, live axle
Carburation	Two SU carburettors		
BHP	36	Brakes	Drums front and rear
Transmission	Four-speed manual gearbox		
		PERFORMANCE	
		Maximum speed	129 km/h (80 mph)
		Fuel consumption	8.07 litres/100 km (35 mpg)

1933 M.G. K3 Magnette

M.G. K3 Magnette

The K3 represents the ultimate pre-war M.G. racing machine, and the most famous of the marque's cars. It was derived from the Magnette range of six-cylinder cars: more expensive versions of the Magna with revised engines, wider track, larger brakes and improved steering. The K-series Magnettes were available in two sizes, and the K3 used the chassis of the shorter version – which was almost exactly the same as that of a Magna. The Magna's engine was reworked for the K3 in short-stroke form with a cross-flow cylinder head, and was highly tuned with supercharging. Most of the 33 K3s built between 1932 and 1934 featured J2-style bodywork for minimum weight and all were fitted with the preselector four-speed gearboxes so fashionable in racing at that time. The idea of this gearbox was that the driver selected the ratio needed with a hand lever before entering a corner and then engaged it by a foot pedal at the appropriate time, leaving both hands free to cope with a wildly swinging steering wheel! The K3 was even faster than the J4 Midget and easier to handle because of its wider track and longer wheelbase.

It achieved countless successes in competition, setting a new hill-climb record in the 1933 Monte Carlo Rally before going on to dominate its class and take the team award in Italy's fabulous 1600 km (1,000 mile) road race, the Mille Miglia, in the same year. The M.G. drivers' success was such that they received a royal reception on the return to England.

More victories followed before the legendary Tazio Nuvolari, the greatest racing driver of the time, took the wheel of a K3 in the 1933 Tourist Trophy race. He broke his class lap record no less than seven times during a thrilling duel with 'Hammy' Hamilton's J4, the Magnette winning by a scant 40 seconds! Nuvolari's winning time remained the fastest in the Tourist Trophy until 1951 when it took Stirling Moss to beat it in a 3.4-litre Jaguar. In 1933, a single-seater version of the K3 won the Brooklands 500-mile race for Eddie Hall, before Ronnie Horton and Capt. George Eyston – one of the Mille Miglia heroes – followed suit with another single-seater in the same year. Eyston's 'Magic Magnette' had two bodies, one for road racing and one more streamlined for record breaking. In this more slippery guise it went on to smash numerous world speed records.

ENGINE		CHASSIS	
Type	M.G. in-line, water-cooled	Frame	Twin side members, cross members
No. of cylinders	6	Wheelbase mm	2214
Bore/stroke mm	57 × 71	Track – front mm	1219
Displacement cc	1087	Track – rear mm	1219
Valve operation	Overhead camshaft	Suspension – front	Half-elliptic springs, beam axle
Sparkplugs per cyl.	1		
Compression ratio	5.4:1 to 6.6:1, according to tune	Suspension – rear	Half-elliptic springs, live axle
Carburation	1 SU carburettor with Powerplus or Marshall supercharger	Brakes	Drums front and rear
		PERFORMANCE	
BHP	105 to 125 according to tune	Maximum speed	177 km/h (110 mph)
		Fuel consumption	18.83 litres/100 km (15 mpg)
Transmission	Preselector four-speed gearbox		

1934 M.G. NA Magnette

M.G. NA Magnette

The NA Magnette, of which 738 were built between 1934 and 1936, was an important car because it was the first M.G. to have a new chassis with its side members wider at the back than at the front – a considerable departure from the earlier pure ladder type. It was also the last of the small six-cylinder M.G.s, besides being the last of the single overhead camshaft cars to stay in production.

The engine was a more highly developed version of the earlier KD Magnette unit of 1271 cc, although M.G. claimed it had a capacity of 1286 cc to distinguish it from the superficially similar, but much less powerful, Wolseley Hornet motor. The change of capacity was achieved by adding one millimetre to the official stroke measurement and caused a great deal of confusion for several decades. The modifications to make this engine superior to that of the Wolseley were extensive: a new cylinder block, cylinder head, inlet manifold, lubrication system and clutch. This was a period when technical development ran riot at Abingdon.

The four-speed manual gearbox fitted to the NA Magnette was similar to the earlier L-type Magna's, although at first it had trials-style ratios of two low – for starting in tricky circumstances – and two much higher, for road work. However the gap between the two sets of ratios proved something of a handicap in normal use, so they were changed for a closer set during the production run, and the new model was called the NB: another example of how M.G.'s constant quest for improvement cut into profits.

Outriggers at each side and the back of the new frame carried the body, insulated from road noise and vibration by Silentbloc rubber-bonded bushes.

The bodywork was typical of the open two- or four-seater type, with the earlier slab tank covered by a more shapely tail. But the Allingham coachbuilding firm also marketed its own two/four-seater tourer with a dickey (or occasional) seat on the NA chassis, alongside an exceptionally pretty Airline fixed-head coupé. Further variants included the ND, which was an N-type Magnette fitted with K2 Magnette slab-tank two-seater body left over from an earlier production run! It had been the K2, in fact, which had formed the basis of the supercharged K3 racing car.

ENGINE		CHASSIS	
Type	M.G. in-line, water-cooled	Frame	Twin side members, cross members
No. of cylinders	6	Wheelbase mm	2438
Bore/stroke mm	57 × 83	Track – front mm	1143
Displacement cc	1271	Track – rear mm	1143
Valve operation	Overhead camshaft	Suspension – front	Half-elliptic springs, beam axle
Sparkplugs per cyl.	1		
Compression ratio	6.2:1	Suspension – rear	Half-elliptic springs, live axle
Carburation	Two SU carburettors		
BHP	56.6	Brakes	Drums front and rear
Transmission	Four-speed manual gearbox		
		PERFORMANCE	
		Maximum speed	129 km/h (80 mph)
		Fuel consumption	8.56 litres/100 km (33 mpg)

1934 M.G. NA Magnette supercharged

M.G. NA Magnette supercharged

The supercharged NA Magnette owned by long-time M.G. enthusiast Mike Allison is an exceptionally interesting car, in that it is an ex-works competition model driven in the 1935 Monte Carlo Rally by Humfrey Symons and Abingdon mechanic Freddie Kindell. In many ways the NA represented a touring version of a K3 and proved outstandingly competitive, finally crashing while vying for the lead of the world's premier rally. It was also one of the works' final experiments with supercharging for a road-equipped car. One of the reasons for abandoning this system of gaining more power was a ban on supercharging for the 1934 Tourist Trophy race that came into force soon after the Symons' car was built.

Subsequently seven more N-type Magnettes were built for competition with highly-tuned, but non-supercharged, engines. They had far more extreme valve timing which filled their combustion chambers well, but promoted a rather rough tick-over. Practically everything else in the engine was uprated so that they could run up to 7000 rpm and produce around 74 bhp – midway between a standard and a supercharged N-type engine. Special bodies with two staggered seats also had to be built for the race;

these close relatives to the now outlawed supercharged NA were called the NE Magnette.

Three of the cars were entered for the TT as a works team for Capt. George Eyston, Wal Handley and Charlie Dodson. Despite sundry panics in the pits, they were soon battling for the lead against much larger cars: a Bentley driven by Eddie Hall and the Lagonda of Brian Lewis. The larger cars could lap faster, but were handicapped on time and consumed more rubber. Dodson built up a lead of just over two minutes during the Bentley's last pit stop and in the relentless pursuit that resulted he had the crowds on tiptoes as the M.G. hung on to win by just 17 seconds.

The ban on supercharging meant that Nuvolari's K3 records were to stand for years and left fans with an intriguing speculation: had the supercharged NA been allowed to compete it would surely have won Britain's oldest road race, and had its crew had more luck, it might have won the world's greatest rally in the following winter. More importantly, though, it was a much more pleasant car to drive than the NE Magnette, which had an engine that was permanently on the ragged edge of tuning.

ENGINE		CHASSIS	
Type	M.G. in-line, water-cooled	Frame	Twin side members, cross members
No. of cylinders	6	Wheelbase mm	2440
Bore/stroke mm	57 × 83	Track – front mm	1140
Displacement cc	1271	Track – rear mm	1140
Valve operation	Overhead camshaft	Suspension – front	Half-elliptic springs, beam axle
Sparkplugs per cyl.	1		
Compression ratio	5.4:1	Suspension – rear	Half-elliptic springs, live axle
Carburation	1 SU carburettor with supercharger	Brakes	Drums front and rear
BHP	Approx. 100	PERFORMANCE	
Transmission	Four-speed manual gearbox	Maximum speed	161 km/h (100 mph)
		Fuel consumption	16.62 litres/100 km (17 mpg)

1934 M.G. PA Midget Cream Cracker

M.G. PA Midget Cream Cracker

The P-type Midget introduced in 1934 featured several fundamental improvements to the J2 and went on to sell a healthy 2000 examples. This Midget had a similar, slightly scaled-down chassis to the N-type Magnette with the same powerful brakes and a new engine with three main bearings to alleviate the problem of broken crankshafts. The extra drag of the additional main bearing reduced the power a little but made the new engine much smoother in operation and so able to withstand a great deal more tuning. The PA Midget (which was followed by 526 PBs) also had a better clutch, gearbox and final drive than the J-types. Its body was similar, but a little roomier and more comfortable.

It was during 1934 that sporting trials reached a height of popularity. Car manufacturers were not supposed to support works teams – so that private competitors had a fair chance – but the events were so prestigious that most of them did. M.G. backed three drivers to the hilt in 1934, providing them with new PA Midgets painted in the works colours of brown and cream. They soon became known as the Cream Crackers (because they really got cracking), with Maurice 'The Colonel' Toulmin in the leading car, which is illustrated here.

At this point the cars retained their normally aspirated 847 cc engines with modifications confined to drastic weight saving. Among the items that had to go were the long sweeping Magnette-style wings that had been introduced on the later J2s; they were replaced with the lighter cycle-type wings originally used. One of the Cream Crackers was later fitted with a Centric supercharger and won the 1935 Brighton-Beer trial for Archie MacDermid, although Toulmin's PA also managed to climb a new 'terror' hill – Widlake.

Another team of Midgets was prepared for the 1936 season using the newly introduced PB engine. This had a larger capacity (939 cc) for more power, with a close-ratio gearbox. When fitted to a Cream Cracker, it was equipped with a belt-driven Marshall supercharger and extensive modifications were made to the running gear. These Cream Crackers ran alongside other works teams including the Three Musketeers, using Magnettes, and were later replaced with 1700 cc cars based on the new T-series Midget. The earlier P-type Cream Crackers, though, remained the most famous of all, and are among those remembered with most affection by M.G. fans.

ENGINE		CHASSIS	
Type	M.G. in-line, water-cooled	**Frame**	Twin side members, cross members
No. of cylinders	4	**Wheelbase mm**	2223
Bore/stroke mm	57 × 83	**Track – front mm**	1067
Displacement cc	847	**Track – rear mm**	1067
Valve operation	Overhead camshaft	**Suspension – front**	Half-elliptic springs, beam axle
Sparkplugs per cyl.	1		
Compression ratio	6.2:1	**Suspension – rear**	Half-elliptic springs, live axle
Carburation	Two SU carburettors		
BHP	34.9	**Brakes**	Drums front and rear
Transmission	Four-speed manual gearbox		
		PERFORMANCE	
		Maximum speed	129 km/h (80 mph)
		Fuel consumption	7.43 litres/100 km (38 mpg)

1937 M.G. TA Midget

M.G. TA Midget

When the axe fell on M.G.'s incredibly complex range, Kimber managed to get approval to design a new Midget to replace both the P-type and the Magnette. This would be the T-series with new dimensions that fell halfway between those of the earlier cars and carried a much roomier body along the lines of the Midget it replaced. For the new car M.G. was forced to use a number of standard Nuffield components to improve the profit margin, so the company opted for the biggest engine it was allowed to fit: a 1293 cc four-cylinder pushrod unit from the Morris Ten saloon. This was not as efficient as the PB's unit, having been developed from the original Bullnose engine, but had the advantage of a larger capacity.

The chassis of the new TA, as it was called, had softer suspension, in keeping with saloon car trends, and the newfangled hydraulic brakes. The TA weighed 45 kg (100 lb) more than the PB, but it was 90 kg (200 lb) lighter than the ND Magnette, and the engine produced 50 bhp, so it was just as fast as the models it replaced. The only problem was that it did not do it in such style!

But the new engine had much more torque than the PB and this made the TA easier to drive. M.G. enthusiasts were dismayed at first by the wholesale changes, but their loyalty to the marque outweighed their almost masochistic affection for the PB. And once they tried the new 'soft and silent' Midget they were amazed to discover that it went just as well. It was the start of the immortal T-series that was to blaze an export trail for M.G., particularly in the United States, and take Abingdon to the threshold of mass production, 3,003 models being built between 1936 and 1939.

The deceptively good performance of the TA was emphasized by the success of a team of slightly modified examples which competed under Cream Cracker colours. They dominated the 1937 trials season with few changes other than aluminium-panelled bodies and cycle-type wings. Later they received 1708 cc engines based on the larger M.G. VA unit, to defend their national team title in 1938. The red-painted Musketeers also ran supercharged TAs as an alternative, with a third team based in Scotland running blue cars under the banner of the Blue Bustards. Later the TA's appeal was extended to include a far more luxurious drop-head coupé built from 1938 onwards. This Tickford-built model was more nearly a direct replacement for the Magnette, as well as being a roomier and more comfortable car to drive.

ENGINE		CHASSIS	
Type	M.G. in-line, water-cooled	Frame	Twin side members, cross members
No. of cylinders	4	Wheelbase mm	2388
Bore/stroke mm	63.5 × 102	Track – front mm	1143
Displacement cc	1292	Track – rear mm	1143
Valve operation	Pushrod	Suspension – front	Half-elliptic springs, live axle
Sparkplugs per cyl.	1		
Compression ratio	7:1	Suspension – rear	Half-elliptic springs, beam axle
Carburation	Two SU carburettors		
BHP	52.4	Brakes	Drums front and rear
Transmission	Four-speed manual gearbox		
		PERFORMANCE	
		Maximum speed	129 km/h (80 mph)
		Fuel consumption	7.85 litres/100 km (36 mpg)

1938 M.G. SA saloon

M.G. SA saloon

The M.G. SA was a car that suffered from internal politics, and deserved to sell more than the 2,738 made between 1936 and 1939. It was also unlucky in that it met exceptionally stiff competition from a brilliant new rival, the SS Jaguar. Leonard Lord was now in charge of M.G. and had identified a healthy market for relatively cheap luxury sports saloons. He thought that all was necessary to sell them in large numbers was to fit an M.G. radiator grille to his existing Wolseley Super Six. Kimber persuaded him that this was not the case, and was eventually allowed to design an exceptionally attractive new body, although the car had to remain a Wolseley under its skin. It was a good deal larger than its recent M.G. predecessor, the KN Magnette, but it was cheaper and therefore seemed extraordinarily good value.

Ironically, the Two-Litre, or SA, suffered from the very inefficiency within the Nuffield Organization that Lord was trying to eradicate. Far too many people were involved in decisions affecting the group's cars with the result that new models were frequently delayed. The prototype SA, first seen in 1935, went through numerous detail changes to use the same parts as Wolseley, which was also changing its cars at the time!

But the biggest blow was the introduction on the SS Jaguar of a powerful new 2663 cc engine. This car was very good looking and performed so well that M.G. realised, too late, that it had underestimated this emergent marque. The Jaguar's designer, William Lyons, ran his business in a thoroughly autocratic manner, so the car went into production without delay in 1936, while the Nuffield Organization was still debating the SA's final specification. This process was not helped by a last-minute change in capacity to 2288 cc to counter the Jaguar's performance. This sort of modification would have been done in only a few days when M.G. was independent, but it took months now and the readily available Jaguar scooped sales that might have been the SA's. Nevertheless, when production of the SA eventually got into full swing, it sold well with a smaller – VA – version being introduced in 1937, and a larger – WA – in 1938. These cars were also offered with Tickford drophead coupé bodywork in 1938 like the one available on the TA, as well as in an alternative open tourer style. The full range, as eventually offered, was in its own way every bit as competitively priced as the S.S. Jaguars; sadly, though, the war prevented the range reaching its full sales potential.

ENGINE		CHASSIS	
Type	M.G. in-line, water-cooled	Frame	Twin side members, cross members
No. of cylinders	6	Wheelbase mm	3124
Bore/stroke mm	Early 69 × 102, later 69.5 × 102	Track – front mm	1356
		Track – rear mm	1356
Displacement cc	Early 2288, later 2322	Suspension – front	Half-elliptic springs, beam axle
Valve operation	Overhead, pushrod		
Sparkplugs per cyl.	1	Suspension – rear	Half-elliptic springs, live axle
Compression ratio	Approx. 6.5:1		
Carburation	Two SU carburettors	Brakes	Drums front and rear
BHP	75		
Transmission	Four-speed manual gearbox	PERFORMANCE	
		Maximum speed	129 km/h (80 mph)
		Fuel consumption	16.61 litres/100 km (17 mpg)

1946 M.G. TC Midget

M.G. TC Midget

The TC was the car that, more than any other, pioneered the great export boom that turned Abingdon into the biggest sports car factory in the world. It emerged as a slightly modernized version of the TB, of which 379 were made in 1939 before war was declared. The main difference between the TB and the TA was that the new car had a much better engine, which had been introduced for a later Morris Ten saloon. This four-cylinder, 1250 cc unit, code-named XPAG, was of far more modern design. It still had the cheaper pushrods, but proved to be exceptionally well suited for tuning to give extra power. Because it had a larger bore, the XPAG engine revved more easily and a lower rear axle ratio could be fitted, which – when combined with the VA's closer gearbox ratios – made the TB much livelier than the TA.

Once the war was over, the priority in 1945 was to make as many cars as possible. The demand was such that anything sold, and it was prudent to concentrate on just one model, rather than to become involved in the complications of producing several. To save time designing a more modern version of their best-seller, the Midget, Abingdon launched straight into producing a TB with a simplified, fully shackled, rear suspension to make servicing easier, and a slightly wider body – the same width as the Tickford coupé, which was discontinued. This was the TC, of which 10,002 were sold by late 1949. In this way, M.G. was able to produce this Midget more than twice as quickly as any previous model.

Although the design of the TC was beginning to look antiquated, orders were strong because the car was readily available. M.G. was able to obtain the steel it needed to produce so many TCs – while many other manufacturers were denied supplies – because a large proportion of the cars were exported. They sold especially well in America, where servicemen returning from the war in Europe wanted to demonstrate how well travelled they were compared to those who had known only Detroit iron. Some customers bought the TC as a second car because it was a complete contrast to the large American family saloon; others because they simply liked British sports cars. Back home in Britain, many people wanted the TC because it was unashamedly pre-war in concept and construction, and it reminded them of better times. But everybody loved it for being the most traditional of sports cars.

ENGINE		CHASSIS	
Type	M.G. in-line, water-cooled	Frame	Twin side members, cross members
No. of cylinders	4	Wheelbase mm	2388
Bore/stroke mm	66.5 × 90	Track – front mm	1143
Displacement cc	1250	Track – rear mm	1143
Valve operation	Overhead, pushrod	Suspension – front	Half-elliptic springs, beam axle
Sparkplugs per cyl.	1		
Compression ratio	7:1	Suspension – rear	Half-elliptic springs, live axle
Carburation	Two SU carburettors		
BHP	54.4	Brakes	Drums front and rear
Transmission	Four-speed manual gearbox		
		PERFORMANCE	
		Maximum speed	126 km/h (78 mph)
		Fuel consumption	9.42 litres/100 km (30 mpg)

1952 M.G. TD Midget

M.G. TD Midget

Although the TD looks very similar to a TC when compared to today's cars, it represented a considerable step forward at the time and was regarded as a thoroughly modern car. Its concept dated back to before the war, when Abingdon designer Syd Enever and Morris suspension expert Alec Issigonis worked on an M.G. version of the Morris Ten saloon. This car, intended for introduction in 1941, had the advanced independent front suspension and an excellent new chassis. The project was revived after the war as the M.G. Y-type saloon, which went into production in 1947. This was a comely, if rather heavy, little car which was selling well, when it became vital to update the TC as other manufacturers managed to get more modern models on the market.

Abingdon responded to these market pressures in the most economical way by shortening the Y-series chassis to about the same dimensions as those of the TC. The still-advanced wishbone-and-coil front suspension gave it a much softer, more positive, ride and helped handling on the rough roads that still abounded in export markets. The steering was made more precise by using a

rack and pinion, which had a great advantage of being readily adapted for left-hand-drive.

The chassis rails were also swept up over the rear axle, rather than beneath it. This gave the rear suspension more room to even out the bumps. A new body was fitted that followed the same traditional lines as the TC, but it was made wider to meet the demands of an American market that had been brought up on far bigger cars. The front suspension changes made it easier and more economical to fit smaller steel disc wheels in place of the glorious old wires that graced the TC. Abingdon was convinced, at that time, that customers would soon go off the nostalgic, racy, wire wheels when they realised how much easier it was to clean the new ones. The wings were reshaped to cover the wider track and smaller wheels and, along with bumpers (fenders) to meet popular demand in America, gave the new TD a very different appearance. Although the styling was still dated, the M.G. Midget had achieved such a good reputation throughout the world that the TD sold in still larger numbers, 29,664 being built between 1949 and late 1953.

ENGINE		CHASSIS	
Type	M.G. in-line, water-cooled	**Frame**	Twin side members, cross members
No. of cylinders	4	**Wheelbase mm**	2388
Bore/stroke mm	66.5 × 90	**Track – front mm**	1143
Displacement cc	1250	**Track – rear mm**	1143
Valve operation	Overhead, pushrod	**Suspension – front**	Half-elliptic springs, beam axle
Sparkplugs per cyl.	1		
Compression ratio	7:1	**Suspension – rear**	Half-elliptic springs, live axle
Carburation	Two SU carburettors		
BHP	54.4	**Brakes**	Drums front and rear
Transmission	Four-speed manual gearbox		
		PERFORMANCE	
		Maximum speed	126 km/h (78 mph)
		Fuel consumption	9.42 litres/100 km (30 mpg)

1955 M.G. TF Midget 1500

M.G. TF Midget 1500

The TF was the last of a line of M.G. Midgets which had started with the J-series. Although it was merely a stopgap before M.G.'s first genuine post-war sports car, it has been heralded as the prettiest Midget ever made. That it should be so acclaimed is almost miraculous when one considers its development. Abingdon foremen Cecil Cousins and Alec Hounslow 'cobbled up' the body in desperation when the square-rigged lines of the TD were presenting a real problem for the salesmen. Only then, after general manager John Thornley had won approval for this very economical facelift, were drawings taken from the prototype and the rebodied TD put into production. The TF's beauty of line was achieved by lowering the TD's scuttle slightly and reducing the radiator height by 96 mm (3½ inches). The radiator was concealed behind a grille which sloped back and the front wings were restyled with faired-in headlights. The rear end received the same sort of attention to detail, and overall the car was lower by 13 mm (½ inch).

Naturally, with such a reduction in frontal area, the TF was quicker than the TD. However acceleration remained much the same until a new 1500 cc engine was installed, developed for the M.G. Magnette introduced in 1953. The saloon got priority for the new power unit, however, and the first year's production of the 9,600 TFs made between 1953 and 1955 had the old XPAG unit. All the TFs had a redesigned interior, which was positively slick when compared to the TD. This had a sloping facia panel with centrally grouped octagon-shrouded instruments, shelves for the personal possessions of both driver and passenger, and a fitted radio. A concealed windscreen wiper motor still allowed the screen to fold flat in the true Midget tradition. Flashing indicators became standard, and wire wheels were again listed as a readily available optional extra in response to cries of outrage from the purists who could not stand the sight of saloon car wheels on a traditional sports car. By the mid-1950s, however, the TF, even in 1500 form, had been left behind on performance by such competitors as the Austin-Healey 100 and the Triumph TR2. But that is immaterial now as the TF1500 – of which 3,400 were made – can be seen as the most sought after development of the traditional M.G. Midget.

ENGINE		CHASSIS	
Type	M.G. in-line, water-cooled	Frame	Twin side members, cross members
No. of cylinders	4	Wheelbase mm	2388
Bore/stroke mm	72 × 90	Track – front mm	1203
Displacement cc	1466	Track – rear mm	1268
Valve operation	Overhead, pushrod	Suspension – front	Independent wishbone and coil
Sparkplugs per cyl.	1		
Compression ratio	8.3:1	Suspension – rear	Half-elliptic springs, live axle
Carburation	Two SU carburettors		
BHP	63	Brakes	Drums front and rear
Transmission	Four-speed manual gearbox		
		PERFORMANCE	
		Maximum speed	142 km/h (88 mph)
		Fuel consumption	12.28 litres/100 km (23 mpg)

1956 M.G. ZA Magnette

M.G. ZA Magnette

The post-war saloon car that took over the name Magnette (in mothballs since 1936) was a complete departure from the norm in one way, but just like every other M.G. in others!

When Leonard Lord once again gained control of M.G. with the formation of the British Motor Corporation, he would like to have abolished the marque and concentrated on selling Austins pure and simple. But M.G. had such a magnificent sales record that the magic name could not simply be swept aside. It would be no good trying to pass off Austins with octagonal badges as proper M.G.s – they had to be rather more than that. But M.G.s had always been based on Wolseleys, which were still in the same empire, so there seemed no harm in pursuing this theme. The solution was not to base a new M.G. on the current Austin, but to take Wolseley's new 4/44 bodyshell and have it revised to accept Austin running gear and M.G. trim.

This Wolseley, which had been launched in 1952 with an XPAG engine, represented a complete departure from the company's earlier practice in that it was of thoroughly modern unitary construction; it had no separate chassis, the body itself providing mountings for the engine, gearbox and suspension. This form of construction rapidly became popular in the early 1950s as a far lighter and (when mass-produced) cheaper way of making cars. One of the advantages of this system was that the occupants were able to sit lower – thus improving handling and reducing drag – because they did not have the chassis rails beneath them, just a flat floorpan on which the bodyshell was based.

The new car had independent front suspension and a live rear axle located by a torque arm. This was necessary because rubber bushes were used extensively in the suspension mountings to reduce maintenance. They also alleviated the noise and harshness that would otherwise have been accentuated by the drumming effect of such bodyshells. The Z-series Magnette was an immediate success, particularly as its new B-series Austin engine made it much faster than the Wolseley, and such touches as an octagonal speedometer surround pleased people loyal to the marque. This reincarnation of the Magnette sold 12,754 in ZA form and 23,846 as a slightly more powerful ZB between 1953 and replacement by an Austin-based model in 1958: roughly ten times as many as the Y-series saloons it replaced. This gives some indication of Abingdon's post-war expansion.

ENGINE		CHASSIS	
Type	M.G. in-line, water-cooled	Frame	Unitary construction
No. of cylinders	4	Wheelbase mm	2642
Bore/stroke mm	73.025 × 88.9	Track – front mm	1295
Displacement cc	1489	Track – rear mm	1295
Valve operation	Overhead, pushrod	Suspension – front	Independent wishbone and coil springs
Sparkplugs per cyl.	1		
Compression ratio	8:1	Suspension – rear	Half-elliptic springs, live axle
Carburation	Two SU carburettors		
BHP	60	Brakes	Drums front and rear
Transmission	Four-speed manual gearbox		
		PERFORMANCE	
		Maximum speed	116 km/h (72 mph)
		Fuel consumption	8.31 litres/100 km (34 mpg)

1959 MGA 1600 roadster

MGA 1600 roadster

When at last M.G. was allowed to introduce its first wholly post-war two-seater, it promptly sold more than 100,000 and became one of the most popular sports cars ever made. It followed the lines of the prototype which had been in existence since 1951, finally making its sporting debut at Le Mans in 1955. The three cars entered used the chassis developed for a record-breaking car run by Capt. George Eyston the previous year, with engines and running gear similar to those used in the new Magnette saloon. These components had already been tested in racing Magnettes. Two of the new MGAs finished the gruelling 24-hour race, but their competition career was cut short by the world's worst motor racing accident at the French circuit that year. Following this, works participation in sport was decidedly limited for several years.

Sales of the production car soared now that an M.G. had a modern all-enveloping body, achieved without jeopardizing the customary Abingdon virtues of low cost, excellent handling and well-nigh unbreakable mechanical components that were good for 160 km/h (100 mph).

More than 50,000 of these early 1500 cc cars were built before the engine capacity was raised to nearly 1600 cc in keeping with the Austin saloon on which they were based. The MGA was hardly altered in any other way, however, and it is a 1600 cc roadster that is illustrated. A total of 31,507 of these machines was made before the engine capacity was raised again to 1622 cc in common again with the Austin saloon. This model was subsequently called the Mark II and remained in production until 1962.

Throughout the model's life it was produced with either the open roadster bodywork or as a pretty fixed-head coupé that was meant to be a budget-priced version of Jaguar's highly successful XK120 coupé. During the period 1958 to 1960, it was also possible to buy an MGA with a twin cam engine, disc brakes and competition wheels as a separate model, again either in open or closed form. The 1588 cc engines used in these cars were unique to M.G. and suffered from a lack of funds for development, which resulted in unreliability. Such problems kept the sales of this very high-performance car down to just over 2,000. For years, the original pushrod-engined MGAs were among the most practical of sports cars and they more than made up for the twin cam's lack of success in club competitions, especially when the pushrod engine was used in the twin cam chassis for the very rare De Luxe model.

ENGINE		CHASSIS	
Type	M.G. in-line, water-cooled	Frame	Twin side members, cross members
No. of cylinders	4	Wheelbase mm	2388
Bore/stroke mm	75.4 × 88.9	Track – front mm	1203
Displacement cc	1588	Track – rear mm	1230
Valve operation	Overhead, pushrod	Suspension – front	Independent wishbone and coil
Sparkplugs per cyl.	1		
Compression ratio	8.3:1	Suspension – rear	Half-elliptic springs, live axle
Carburation	Two SU carburettors		
BHP	79.5	Brakes	Discs front, drums rear
Transmission	Four-speed manual gearbox		

PERFORMANCE	
Maximum speed	166 km/h (103 mph)
Fuel consumption	10.1 litres/100 km (28 mpg)

1963 M.G. Midget 1098

M.G. Midget 1098

The demise of the M.G. TF Midget in 1955 left a gap in the small sports car market, because the MGA was seen as one step up. So Leonard Lord, with no love for M.G., prompted Donald Healey to build a new version of the Midget based on the Austin A35. Healey's scaled-down Jaguar D type, called the Sprite, was a brilliantly simple car that immediately caught on when it was introduced in 1958. Ironically, it was built at Abingdon alongside the MGA and the larger Austin-Healeys.

Simplicity was the keynote of the Sprite, with a four-cylinder engine that was basically the same as that used in the small Austin, Morris Minor and the new Mini which followed a year later. The only really unusual feature of the 'Frogeye' Sprite, as it was affectionately termed, was its very rounded styling and extraordinary headlights mounted on the bonnet – hence the nickname.

By 1961, BMC had decided that the Frogeye should be brought in line with a corporate styling policy. Those idiosyncratic headlights had to go, and the new car would have to have a luggage boot lid to replace its baggage-loading hold behind the seats. So the Sprite was restyled along the lines of the new MGB which would replace the MGA in 1962. It was given a conventional front with headlights faired into the wings and a new rear end to match, with a proper boot. Apart from that, the Sprite was almost unchanged, with its punt-type floorpan, wishbone and coil front suspension, very sensitive rack and pinion steering that made it as responsive as roller skates, quarter-elliptic rear springs and live axle. Like the MGA, it had extremely reliable mechanical components and it was exceptionally cheap to run, with low maintenance costs and excellent fuel economy.

Lord had retired by the time the new car was introduced in 1961, and the man who replaced him, George Harriman, was dedicated to badge engineering – producing almost identical cars as different makes, with only badges and trim that were genuinely different. In keeping with this policy, two versions of the Sprite were produced, one badged as an Austin-Healey and the other as an M.G. Midget. As the years went on, the mechanical components were uprated, the example illustrated having an 1100 cc engine. Between 1958 and 1980, 354,807 of these 'Spridgets', as they were called, were produced, including 9,601 M.G. Midget 1100 Mark Is.

ENGINE		CHASSIS	
Type	M.G. in-line, water-cooled	Frame	Unitary construction
No. of cylinders	4	Wheelbase mm	2030
Bore/stroke mm	65 × 84	Track – front mm	1160
Displacement cc	1098	Track – rear mm	1140
Valve operation	Overhead, pushrod	Suspension – front	Independent wishbone and coil
Sparkplugs per cyl.	1		
Compression ratio	8.9:1	Suspension – rear	Quarter-elliptic springs, live axle
Carburation	Two SU carburettors	Brakes	Discs front, drums rear
BHP	56		
Transmission	Four-speed manual gearbox		
		PERFORMANCE	
		Maximum speed	142 km/h (88 mph)
		Fuel consumption	8.07 litres/100 km (35 mpg)

1967 MGB roadster

MGB roadster

More than half a million MGBs were made between 1962 and 1980 to fulfil the need for a cheap sporting vehicle that was also solid and reliable, and which was available in open, hard top and fixed-head forms, with two seats or a vestigial four. They were cheap to run and thoroughly dependable, yet they were not made in such large quantities as to be overly common. As the MGA's shape was based on Capt. George Eyston's pre-war K3 record car, so the MGB's styling followed the post-war record-breaker EX181, but used the same basic mechanical components as the MGA. The MGB differed from the MGA, however, in that it had a bodyshell of unitary construction like the Magnette saloon. Phenomenal reserves of strength were built into these cars, with the result that many have lasted well beyond the normal lifespan of a sports car.

Following the introduction of the two-seater roadster with an 1800 cc four-cylinder version of the MGA's engine, a fixed-head coupé called the GT was built from 1965. This had two tiny rear seats that were ideal for small children and a hatchback rear door like Aston Martin's DB Mark III to accommodate far larger quantities of luggage than was possible in the roadster.

Try as they might, Abingdon could not reduce the weight of the MGB to that of the MGA without compromising on strength, but the increase in engine capacity restored any performance that would have been lost. The sheer strength of the new bodyshell meant that the spring rates could be reduced, giving the new car a more pleasant ride without any loss of roadholding. The redesigned bodyshell also had an advantage in that it provided more room for the occupants.

It is of interest to note that for the first time on an M.G. roadster, the new car had locks on the doors and boot lid! The lack of locks on earlier models dated back to the time that open cars almost invariably had their hoods down and there was then not much point in locking doors. The same theory applied to the luggage area because baggage on previous Midgets had normally been carried strapped to a rack on the fuel tank. A notable optional extra that became available in 1963 was an overdrive that reduced fuel consumption and made the MGB far less frenetic while cruising at high speed. Production figures for the Mark I model illustrated were 115,898 roadsters and 21,835 GTs.

ENGINE		CHASSIS	
Type	M.G. in-line, water-cooled	Frame	Unitary construction
No. of cylinders	4	Wheelbase mm	2311
Bore/stroke mm	80 × 89	Track – front mm	1245
Displacement cc	1798	Track – rear mm	1250
Valve operation	Overhead, pushrod	Suspension – front	Independent wishbone and coil
Sparkplugs per cyl.	1		
Compression ratio	8.8:1	Suspension – rear	Half-elliptic springs, live axle
Carburation	Two SU carburettors		
BHP	95	Brakes	Discs front, drums rear
Transmission	Four-speed manual gearbox or manual and overdrive		
		PERFORMANCE	
		Maximum speed	171 km/h (106 mph)
		Fuel consumption	10.46 litres/100 km (27 mpg)

1973 MGB GT V8

MGB GT V8

The MGB GT V8 was the first truly successful attempt at producing a really high-performance road-going M.G. It used a V8 engine that Rover had started manufacturing under licence from General Motors in 1967. Rover was absorbed into British Leyland the following year but the engine did not find its way into an M.G. immediately. There were many other vehicles in the British Leyland range that needed it, especially the saloons made by Rover who had found it in the first place. This meant that M.G.'s designs on the V8 took a back seat until a private firm started using it in MGB conversions in 1970. These Costello MGBs received such acclaim that British Leyland had to follow suit with the MGB GT V8 in 1972. Following the disaster with the MGC, an absolute minimum was spent on development – but the car hardly needed it. The new V8 weighed about the same as the B-series engine and could be 'shoehorned' into the bodyshell with only a few modifications. It was soon mated to an MGB gearbox with a higher rear axle ratio to give even better performance than the MGC, with handling every bit as good as the normal MGB. The V8 power unit was confined to the GT bodyshell because it produced so much torque that it was thought that the roadster could not cope with it.

Several problems faced the new V8, however: British Leyland was in severe financial difficulties by 1972 and could not afford to have it adapted to meet emission regulations in its biggest market, the United States; the fuel consumption looked like being too high with the emission equipment installed; and General Motors had always seen the MGB as a competitor for their range of Corvette sports cars. In Europe, the new V8 faced very stiff competition from the Ford Capri 3-litre which was lighter because it had been designed as a fixed-head coupé from the start and offered better rear seat accommodation. And no sooner had the new V8 gone into production than the world was plunged into an energy crisis, and it became simply unfashionable to be seen driving a fast, thirsty, car. Production continued at a low key until 1976 when British Leyland were set to concentrate on a V8-engined version of the Triumph TR7. By then 2,591 MGB GT V8s had been built: they still remain the fastest M.G.s ever made and among the most pleasant.

If only M.G. could have had the Rover engine in time for the stiffer MGC bodyshell in 1967, they could have had that world-beater!

ENGINE		CHASSIS	
Type	Rover V8, water-cooled	Frame	Unitary construction
No. of cylinders	8	Wheelbase mm	2311
Bore/stroke mm	89 × 71	Track – front mm	1245
Displacement cc	3528	Track – rear mm	1250
Valve operation	Overhead, hydraulic tappets, pushrods	Suspension – front	Independent wishbone and coil
Sparkplugs per cyl.	1	Suspension – rear	Half-elliptic springs, live axle
Compression ratio	8.25:1	Brakes	Discs front, drums rear
Carburation	Two SU carburettors		
BHP	137	**PERFORMANCE**	
Transmission	Four-speed manual gearbox and overdrive	Maximum speed	201 km/h (125 mph)
		Fuel consumption	11.3 litres/100 km (25 mpg)

1980 MGB roadster

MGB roadster

During its early years there were constant complaints about the massive black bumpers that had to be fitted to MGBs, including the V8, to comply with American safety regulations in 1974. It has been only in recent years that owners have appreciated them for the protection they give to valuable coachwork. Considering the problems involved Abingdon did a good styling job. The monstrous bumpers were fitted to meet Californian legislation which decreed that new cars should suffer no harm from a 8 km/h (5 mph) impact – even against a concrete block. This entailed fitting reinforced steel beams front and rear to support the dodgem-car style bumpers, adding 127 mm (5 in) to the overall length and 31.75 kg (70 lb) in weight just where it was not needed.

When it comes to handling, a car's body can be viewed as a pendulum and the last place extra weight is needed is at either end. Even worse, the ride height was raised by 38 mm (1½ in) to save having to redesign the bodyshell completely to meet new bumper-height regulations, with little done to counter the resultant strong roll oversteer. It became a classic case of legislation aimed at reducing accident injury causing the car to become less safe because its makers could not afford to redesign it completely,

even if there had been time. In addition, the engine had to be detuned by 25 bhp to meet new emission regulations, which, combined with the extra weight, reduced the performance of American examples. Non-American MGBs were unchanged.

The roadholding was improved greatly in 1976, however, by fitting an anti-roll bar at the rear. The interior was also redesigned and happily many of the features were eliminated which had begun to seem very dated as other manufacturers brought out new cars during the MGB's long production run.

The pedals were remounted to make proper 'heeling and toeing' possible, the cubbyhole in the dashboard had the ignition key lock removed which meant that it could be opened without switching off the engine, and the seats were given cloth trimming – although there was still a school of thought that yearned for the very expensive leather seats that had graced earlier MGBs. In many ways, the MGB made in 1980 was the best of the 'rubber-bumper' models, and being the youngest is still in great demand, mainly because it is often in so much better condition than old ones. By 1980, the people who bought them new had learned to appreciate the MGB as one of the last of the real sports cars.

ENGINE		CHASSIS	
Type	M.G. in-line, water-cooled	Frame	Unitary construction
No. of cylinders	4	Wheelbase mm	2311
Bore/stroke mm	80.26 × 88.9	Track – front mm	1245
Displacement cc	1798	Track – rear mm	1250
Valve operation	Overhead, pushrod	Suspension – front	Independent wishbone and coil springs
Sparkplugs per cyl.	1		
Compression ratio	8:1	Suspension – rear	Half-elliptic springs, live axle
Carburation	Two SU carburettors		
BHP	88	Brakes	Discs front, drums rear
Transmission	Four-speed manual gearbox and overdrive		
		PERFORMANCE	
		Maximum speed	164 km/h (102 mph)
		Fuel consumption	11.3 litres/100 km (25 mpg)

1982 MG Metro

MG Metro

In 1980 British Leyland staked everything on the car it hoped would save the company – the new Metro saloon. It was so well received that it fulfilled all expectations, with an MG version in 1982 as a top-of-the-line model. The most striking feature of the Metro was its completely new shape, a hard thing to achieve in the very competitive market for mini hatchbacks. Every other major manufacturer was making them and they frequently looked alike because they were almost totally designed by computer to meet myriad worldwide regulations. The Metro scored by being between 100 and 250 mm (4 to 10 inches) shorter than any of its rivals. This was because it retained the original Mini layout of having its gearbox directly beneath the engine – which was similar to that used in the M.G. Midgets – whereas its rivals invariably had their gearboxes alongside. This extraordinarily compact configuration gave the Metro an exceptionally big cabin for its overall size and with a down-sloping bonnet it had that cheeky appeal not seen in a BMC or British Leyland car since the Mini of 1959. Excellent handling was ensured by placing one wheel at each corner with hardly any overhanging bodywork – quite the opposite to the black-

bumper M.G.s. The suspension was by well-tried Hydragas units which were quite acceptable for normal use but needed to be made much stiffer for competition.

More than 20 years of development in its transverse location had made sure there were no snags in the 1275 cc engine, and the gearchange was much more refined than on the original Mini. The steering was not quite so direct, but still exceptionally responsive, making the MG Metro feel very much like the renowned Mini Cooper of old.

To quote *CAR* magazine: 'Like all the best cars, the MG Metro has a co-ordinated balance of qualities that tally with human actions and reactions, comparable to a top-grade tennis racquet or a competition class aerobatic plane. Its responses are quick as lightning, accurate and predictable, and there are no traps or pitfalls to catch out the driver with his defences down.'

As if that was not enough to excite M.G. enthusiasts, a far faster version was waiting in the wings. The MG Metro Turbo was introduced late in 1982 with 93 bhp and a top speed of 180 km/h (112 mph) to make it the fastest MG saloon ever made.

ENGINE		CHASSIS	
Type	M.G. in-line, water-cooled	Frame	Unitary construction
No. of cylinders	4	Wheelbase mm	2251
Bore/stroke mm	71 × 81	Track – front mm	1274
Displacement cc	1275	Track – rear mm	1274
Valve operation	Overhead, pushrod	Suspension – front	Independent unequal length links, Hydragas spring
Sparkplugs per cyl.	1		
Compression ratio	10.5:1	Suspension – rear	Independent trailing arms, Hydragas spring
Carburation	One SU carburettor		
BHP	72		
Transmission	Four-speed manual gearbox	Brakes	Discs front, drums rear
		PERFORMANCE	
		Maximum speed	142 km/h (88 mph)
		Fuel consumption	8.97 litres/100 km (31.5 mpg)